# *i want my groove back! . . .*
# GOD'S WAY

### maxine l. bryant

Dr. Bondage,
You're a fabulous woman
of God -
and He'll keep you in your
stay as/God
GROOVE! you i your

Maxine
2009

# *i want my groove back!* ...
# GOD'S WAY

## maxine l. bryant

**Popular Truth Publishing**
Indianapolis, Indiana

Popular Truth Publishing
anyike@netscape.com

ISBN: 0-9631547-5-3

Cover design by IMMAJN Communications

Edited by
Monique Manning Jones
and
Monifa A. Jumanne, Ph.D.

**Printed in the United States of America**

**Bible translations used:**

**King James Version**
**New Living Translation**
**New American Standard**

# DEDICATION

This book is dedicated to women everywhere
who find themselves living in a
place of non-groove.


In memory of my friend
Damon Jones (1948-2002)
who constantly reminded
me to stay in my groove!

# CONTENTS

# ACKNOWLEDGMENTS

I first wish to give praise and thanks to God for the gift of "words" that He has deposited into me. I also thank Him for keeping me through the rough times during which I learned how to get my groove His Way!

I also want to thank four women and one man who read this book in its initial stages and gave me invaluable feedback: Terry Hurston, Denise Hayes, Patrice Peoples, Lori Peterson, and Juard Barnes. I love each of you and appreciate you so much!

In addition, I must give thanks to my editor and sister, Monique Manning Jones. You are a gem and God has to love you much for depositing into you the wonderful gift of "wordsmithing." Speaking of editors, I must also give a special 'thank you' to Dr. Monifa Jumanne for providing the second edit in preparation for the second printing of this book.

Additionally, James C. Anyike, you are the best! Your patience with me through this process has meant so much! The world must know that you are a "publisher extraordinaire!" I'm glad God used Wanda Spann-Roddy to introduce us. Thanks, Wanda!

I would be remiss if I failed to thank "my crew"–my dear friends who loved me before I got my groove and who have an appreciation for my journey. You know who you are and I love each of you deeply.

Additionally, I wish to give a special thanks to the persons whose situations I refer to in the Groove Barometer section of the book. Thanks for allowing me to share your stories!

Finally, I thank my children, Mayosha Martin and Jonathan Bryant, for being my God-given "teachers" of how to get and keep my groove. Throughout our easy times and our rough times, God used both of you to show me how to lean on Him for my groove! I love you both and am ever thankful to God for the privilege and honor of being selected to be your parent!

# POETIC PREFACE

### *i want my groove back!*
*an original poem by Maxine L. Bryant*

*when did i loose it?  where did it go?*
*how can i get it back – you know, my groove thang*

*i can't get my groove on if i don't have my groove!*
*i want my groove back*
*stella got hers           i want mine too!*

*when you got your groove the sun comes up bright and never sets*
*the stars in your eyes sparkle and dance untiringly*
*the sky is always blue and it rains only enough to disperse the*
*        fragrance of the flowers and turn the brown grass green*

*when you got your groove you are queen of your castle and it doesn't*
*        matter if you share your throne with a king or not!*
*your castle is on top of your world and you see everything from a*
*            bird's               eye               view*
*your majestic mountain is nothing less than magical*
*up there the air is thin and crisp and nothing takes your breath away and*
*your attitude is as high as your altitude and you*
*                    feel               good!*

*when you got your groove nothing rains on your parade and your laughter*
*comes from deep within your heart –*
*            not from the tip-toe humor of your court jester*

*i want my groove back*

*i want to feel the wind in my face  the sun on my back        a*
*            sprinkle of good fortune on my head and silk on my feet*
*i want to dance – feet floating on air        defying gravity with*
*            short            sure            steps*

ix

*i want to race effortlessly thru the woods     the desert*

                          *the seashores               the seasons*
*always taking time to take in and appreciate my space and place*

*i want my groove back*

*i alone am responsible for my groove*
                *i can't        i shouldn't         and            i won't*
*depend on you to give me my groove*
      *it's my groove          i lost it           and            i    alone must get it back*
*you see it was mine to begin with*
*i gave it up*
*i surrendered my groove in the never ending negotiation of the*
                          *american dream*
                                        *forget the american dream!*

*i want my groove back and i must search deep within myself to find it*
*i've got to look past the superficial    beyond the surface*
          *thru the screen and    deep inside my shell      and      find my soul*
                      *for therein lies my groove*

*i must do this by myself          with myself          for myself*
*when I find my soul and get my groove back I will be ready to receive*
                          *my soul mate*

*i've got to get my groove back*
*with my groove i can enjoy the essence of myself and i can share my*
                          *whole self with you*

              *i want my groove back – and i'm gonna get it!*

X

# FOREWORD FROM THE AUTHOR

The movie, *How Stella Got Her Groove Back*, had a major impact on me. I could relate so much to the principle character in terms of her finding her groove in a man. I have looked for my groove in men for many years. In fact, unfortunately, many people often look for their groove in other people. However, we eventually learn that real groove can't be found in other people – real groove is found only after looking inward to self and upward to God!

After watching the movie, I was inspired to write the poem, *i want my groove back*. Eventually I developed the poem into a motivational workshop that was designed to help people to begin to heal from the hurt of broken groove and guide them on a journey towards a place of inner groove. I called the workshop "I Want My Groove Back." The workshop was a hit and I received many requests to hold it in cities across Indiana. Once, while facilitating the workshop in Marion, Indiana, a participant came up to me afterwards and informed that I needed to write a book, because the information she learned was too important not to be easily accessed in written form to share with others. I dismissed her, thinking "I don't want to take the time to write a book." However, her words stayed with me, continually nagging me in the back of my mind. After a while, I began revising the handouts and other materials I used in the workshop into more of a narrative form. During this time I continued to find myself falling back into the old familiar habit of searching for my groove in relationships with men. I found myself experiencing challenging financial situations and exasperating situations with my teenage daughter. Even though I was a devout Christian, I allowed these things to move me from my point of groove and began handling things the same way I used to handle them – looking for validation and for my sense of self from others, namely men. At one point, during a time when I was definitely operating out of my groove, God spoke to me and told me that while trying to get my groove back was a worthwhile endeavor, I was going about it the wrong way! You see, the workshop focused on "cute-sy" things like giving yourself positive messages and not giving other people power to take your groove. It was about self-empowerment and self-enhancement. God pointed out to me that true groove cannot be attained without Him! He began to guide me through scripture and showed me the difference between internal and external groove. He showed me the groove imitators and the groove stealers. He pointed out the many times when I, myself, had been fooled—even after writing the poem and developing the workshop. I realized that the only way to obtain real groove is to do it God's way. I put aside the material for the book that I'd written up to that point, and began all over – this time writing what God inspired me to write, the way He inspired me to write it. The process took well over 6 years. The final result was the first printing of *i want my groove back!. . .God's Way.*

The initial printing was designed especially for female readers. However, many men bought and read the book also. They repeatedly told me that the book spoke to them and blessed them in many ways. This prompted my publisher and me to consider revising the book to make it less gender specific. The result is what you are holding.

I truly pray that you are blessed by this book. It blessed me to write it and I still refer to it from time to time when I need to be reminded to remain in my groove and not fall for the groove imitators and not give groove stealers power to take my groove.

Throughout the book I refer to various situations. They are situations that really happened. They all happened to me! The beautiful thing is that God brought me out of each situation and kept me in my groove. He'll keep you in your groove too - just dare to trust Him to do it!

Jabez prayed that he would be "blessed...indeed," that his territory would be enlarged, that the Lord's hand would be with him, and that he would be kept from evil. The Bible tells us that God granted his request. My prayer is that the words from this book will reach out and touch you where you most need to be touched and that your life will be the better as a result of reading these pages. I believe God will grant my request.

Continue to be blessed,

*Maxine*

# i want my groove back!...
# GOD'S WAY

## Introduction – Groovin'

When are you happiest? When are you most at peace? Is it when you are alone? Is it when you and your mate are enjoying special moments? Is it when the children are away? Is it when you have completed a difficult assignment at work? Is it when you have thousands of dollars in the bank? Just when are you in your groove?

Many of us search daily for our groove. At times we may believe we are operating in it. But something happens and we realize that those moments are merely groove imitators! How do you know when you're in your groove? How do you stay there? What do you do when you lose it?

Have you ever been frozen in fear, stuck on stupid, literally lost in love, tormented with troubling relationships, felt disconnected, discombobulated, and dismissed? Has parenting felt more like a burden than a blessing? Have you questioned your own sanity, doubted your own self-worth, wished you were someone else—somewhere else? Do you often feel you're not good enough, not pretty enough, not smart enough, not talented enough, unworthy, unlovable and undeserving? Then you know what it feels like to be out of your groove. I invite you to turn the page, keep reading, and embark upon a journey that can lead you to a state of groove. You don't have to go to Jamaica or hook up with a handsome hunk. Think about it for a moment. Did your last hot and fabulous hook up with a handsome hunk or honey (stateside or seaside) leave you afterwards unfulfilled and empty? That's because your groove can't be truly realized through other people, places, or things. However, it can be

1

found by looking into the Word of God. The following pages will guide you through an exploration of pivotal solutions for non-groove from a Christ-focused perspective. In His Word, God has clearly outlined how we can reclaim our groove.

The poem, "i want my groove back," alludes to an initial step that leads towards the transformation from non-groove to groove. However, to attain a holistic state of groove, you must not only look inside yourself—you must look up toward the Lord! For in Him there is more than enjoyment, there is joy; there is more than happiness, there is fulfillment; there is more than relaxation, there is peace.

So, what are you waiting for? I don't know about you, but I want my groove back—God's way!

# Groove Glossary:

**non-groove**    an inability to trust oneself or others, being overly needy and depending on others for happiness

**groove stealers**    people, places, things, and circumstances that move us from our state of groove—often without our full recognition of it

**groove imitators**    people, places, things, and circumstances that make us feel as if we're operating in our groove, that look like groove, but in actuality are keeping us from reaching our groove

**groovin'**    operating (living, being) in a state of groove

**inner groove**    inner peace resulting from a love relationship with the Lord that does not rely upon external stimuli

**groove**    a peaceful, balanced state of being that is not reliant upon external factors

**groove giver**    God

**groove keeper**    The Holy Spirit

**groove monitor**    The Word of God

# Chapter One:
## Getting in Touch with Feelings of Groove
*"When you got your groove the sun comes up bright and never sets"*

**ℋow do you feel when you have your groove?**

**Happy?  Content?  Satisfied?  Wealthy?
On top of the world?  At peace?  Accomplished?**

Often, when you have a true sense of who you are, where you are going, and why, you may experience feelings of groove. When was the last time you felt that way? What was going on in your life that brought you to a point of feeling centered and at peace? Think back to those moments and relish them for a while. For when you have moved from that place of centeredness, returning to it requires first remembering how you felt when you were there! If you're honest with yourself, you will probably find that inner peace and centeredness happen when you are O.K. with you—regardless of external situations. Inner peace and centeredness are more likely to occur when you are rooted in your love for Christ and His love for you. This is the equivalent to abiding in Christ's love. Jesus instructs us to abide in His love in St. John 15:9. Abiding in the love of Christ guarantees an inner peace that cannot be replicated–no matter what havoc you're going through. The questions are: how do you abide in His love? What does that look like?

Consider Revelations 2:4. Here Christ expresses displeasure with the church at Ephesus with the words, "Thou hast left thy 'first love'." Perhaps an initial question should be, "Who is the first love?" Here Christ is referring to Himself. He is (or should be) your first love. Our sins, our being consumed with our own desires, our lack of faith—all these things separate us from our first love. When we put other people, other things, and other circumstances in front of Christ, we leave our first love. Returning to that first love securely builds the foundation for getting in touch with feelings of groove. Having a true love for Christ enables you to reach down within yourself and begin to love you just because He first loved you! You are only ready to truly love yourself after you have come to terms with your love for Christ and the realization that He loves you in spite of you. The chorus to the song "The Greatest Love of All" reminds us that "Learning to love yourself is the greatest love of all." Many of us truly don't love ourselves. In fact, many of us can't really define what self love is! Oh, we say we love ourselves and we talk about self love. We read books about self love. Indeed, we have become very skillful at fooling others and ourselves. But if we really loved ourselves, we would not engage in the self-destructive behaviors that so frequently plague us. Such behaviors are borne out of poor choices and include: choosing a mate for all the wrong reasons; choosing a job out of desperation instead of taking an inventory of skills and enjoyable tasks; choosing a place of worship without truly seeking spiritual guidance; choosing to have children without really thinking through what is involved with positive parenting; making financial decisions out of emotion instead of realistic figures–the list goes on and on. These are just a few examples of destructive behaviors that result from a lack of self-love. To begin the process of getting your groove back, it is necessary to recognize and identify self-love. Having a love relationship with Christ–abiding in His love–lays the foundation for having a sense of self-love. Earlier I asked two questions: 1) How do you abide in Christ's love and 2) What does that look like? Abiding in Christ's love requires a trust in Him and a level of commitment to Him that few understand. 1 Corinthians 13, often referred to as the 'love chapter', provides an excellent portrait of agape love - a love that loves in spite of, an unconditional love, a self-less love–Christ's love. Take a moment to read 1 Corinthians 13. We can love like that only when we are abiding in the love of Christ and have taken on His characteristics. That kind of love is impossible without Christ.


## BECOMING WHOLE

Each of us operates from a position of dysfunction at some level–that place of not knowing who we really are, unable to trust ourselves and others, not truly loving ourselves, faulty thinking and rationalization. Why do I say that? Because we're human. From the fall of man in the book of Genesis until the very present, mankind has been dysfunctional because of the presence of sin in our lives. The only way to discover functionality is through Christ Jesus! Through Him, we move from being fragmented and dysfunctional towards being whole and functional. Often, in our dysfunction, we may sabotage our own lives and success out of a fear that may not be initially evident. It may be fear of failure, fear of success, fear of rejection, etc. Fear can paralyze us and squarely position us to operate from a position of dysfunction. Perhaps that is why the Apostle Paul tells young Timothy in 2 Timothy 1:7: "For God hath not given us the spirit of fear, but of power, and of love, and of a sound mind." Know that God has given us the spirit of power — power to overcome fear and power to accomplish great things. You do realize that "Greater is He that is in you than he that is in the world" *(1 John 4:4)*. God has also given us the spirit of love — His love. When we accept His love, we are then in position to love ourselves and others.

God demonstrates His love for us in every book of the Bible, from Genesis to Revelation. However, one verse sums up the love of God very well, "Hereby perceive we the love of God, because He laid down His life for us. . ." **(1 John 3:16a)**. The first step towards wholeness is recognizing that God loves you, therefore you can love yourself—not because you're so deserving of being loved, but rather, because you are "fearfully and wonderfully made" and thus, loveable *(Psalm 139:14)*. Once you accept the fact that God loves you in spite of you and not because of you, you can position yourself to begin to love you for the person you are, with all of your imperfections. Only God can show you how to do that. I am in awe with the fact that God knows all about me, yet loves me anyway! Accepting that fact can be difficult for some people. Allow me to share a story:

> Years ago I worked for an agency that provided counseling services to inmates at the Marion County Jail in Indianapolis, Indiana. There I met a woman who had been incarcerated for a while. As we were talking one day, she disclosed that she didn't think God could love her because of the things she had done. I began to pray and ask the Lord to give me guidance as to how I should respond. This is what I said, "God doesn't love us because we deserve to be loved. He loves us because we are His own creation." I then asked her if she loved her adult children who abandoned her once she was arrested. She replied a resounding "Yes!" I asked her why she loved her children. They didn't write or come to visit. They refused her request for commissary money. They had basically cut her off. Yet she still loved them. She responded that she loved them because they were a part of her. She had birthed them and would always love them no matter what they did. Using her own words, I explained that God does the same thing. Each of us is His special creation. Man cannot replicate a sperm or an egg. He can join them

7

together in a test-tube, but he cannot create either one. God is the only creator of sperms and eggs. So every baby born is created by God. Since she was created by God, He loved her just as she loved her children – unconditionally. Guess what? She got it! She recognized that as her creator, God loved her no matter what. In that one visit, that particular woman began to realize that she could forgive herself, accept the love and forgiveness of God, and move on to begin loving herself.

In addition to power and love, God has given us the spirit of a sound mind. A sound mind is one that thinks clearly, makes wise decisions, and operates in a state of functionality (as opposed to dysfunction). No matter what the circumstances are, a sound mind maintains balance through Christ Jesus. In fact, the prophet Isaiah writes, "Thou wilt keep him in perfect peace, whose mind is stayed on thee: because he trusteth in thee" *(Isaiah 26:3)*. Can you trust God to keep you centered—no matter what is going on around you? It may be difficult to truly trust God because you've been disappointed by others you've trusted. You have to remember that God won't let you down—as perhaps others have. Although you may not always understand, for His ways are not our ways and His thoughts are not our thoughts *(Isaiah 55:8),* you can rest assured that God always has your best interest at heart and that He truly cares for you—for you are His creation. You can trust Him to keep you centered in every situation—even when your mind is riddled with unanswered questions and you wonder if you've ever experienced your groove.

**THE QUESTION**

"What if I don't know how it feels to have my groove, because I never experienced having it in the first place?" That is the proverbial question. The fact is that when you are in your groove—you will know it because it is God-given: magnificent and unmistakable. Can you recall a time in your life when, in spite of adverse situations around you, you experienced true peace in the midst of your storm? Perhaps it was when a loved one passed away, and God kissed you with consolation. Perhaps it was when you received a call that your son or daughter had been arrested. God spoke to you with solace and wisdom. Perhaps it was when your mate walked out on you. God touched your heart and reminded you that He wanted to be the love of your life. When you tap into that moment, you are tapping into a moment of groove. Groove is that gift from God that is like a special treat—eating candy apples at the state fair, watching a fresh batch of hot fudge or cotton candy being made, enjoying the sunrise on a bright sunny morning or looking at the stars when the moon is shining bright. That moment, no matter how brief or how long, was a gift from God. Why do I say that? Well, because God gives a gift of peace that "passeth all understanding" *(Philippians 4:7)*. When we experience inner peace, even if for a fleeting moment, even if there is chaos all around us, we are experiencing a moment of groove.

When you've got your groove, your worries do not consume you. You are aware of the cares you may have in this world, but they do not pull you down. They do not incapacitate you. For a moment, you may even feel that the responsibilities of life are suspended in mid-air. This is not disillusionment; this is contentment. This is not avoidance; this is recognizing that life's challenges and responsibilities exist yet refusing to become bogged down with worry and frustration. This is *choosing* to be in a state of groove (o.k., that discussion comes in another chapter!)

9

When you've got your groove, not only do you possess inner peace, but you're positioned to fully operate in your God-given purpose. Many people live out their entire lives not fully knowing or understanding the reason they are here on earth—their God-given purpose. When you're off-center, out of touch with God, out of sorts, out of your groove, you can't easily find your purpose. On the other hand, when you're centered and at peace, you can hear God speak to you and "see" where He's guiding you as He leads you on your "purpose journey". In Chapter Five the concept of purpose is discussed in more detail; however, I want to encourage you here by simply saying that knowing your purpose is critical to living in your groove. Can you identify something that you do well, that you enjoy doing, that you just cannot not do? If you can identify such a thing, that may very well be your purpose. Your purpose may be to sow laughter and joy into other people's lives. It may be to care for the elderly and for young children. Each of us has a purpose to fulfil while we live–both in the spiritual and in the natural realm. Spiritually, we recognize that we are created to worship God. But in the natural, what's your purpose?

Why is it important to get in touch with prior feelings of groove? Good question. And the answer is, that for some of us, it has been a long time since we experienced that place of centeredness. In order to recognize genuine groove when we experience it again, we need to remember how having it once felt. A wise person once said, "You won't get where you're going, if you forget where you've been."

Isolate a moment in time when you were at peace with yourself, a time when you liked yourself and could appreciate and love yourself. That, my friend, is the beginning of your place of groove. You can only truly love yourself if you have the love of Christ within you. When you get in touch with your place of self-love based solely on God's love for you, you have returned to your state of groove.

So go ahead, close your eyes and take a moment to reflect on a time in your life when your groove was in full swing. Give yourself permission to experience *"the wind in your face  the sun on your back  a sprinkle of good fortune on your head and silk on your feet."* This is the first step to getting your groove back. So as Nike says, "Just do it!"

## REFLECTIONS

*Describe a time in your life when you experienced true inner peace.*

_____

_____

_____

_____

_____

*Where were you?  What were you doing?*

_____

_____

_____

*How long ago was it?*

_____

*Reflect on your purpose.  What is it?*

_____

_____

_____

# Chapter Two:
## Who/What Took My Groove?
*"i surrendered my groove in the never-ending negotiation of
the american dream. . ."*

Watch a baby nestle in the arms of a parent. Look at young toddlers
innocently playing in the park. See the wonder in the eyes of a young
child who has just discovered the magnificent scent of a sweet rose.
You are witnessing a moment of groove! Somewhere in our journey
into adulthood, the innocent groove of our childhood is replaced with
the hustle and bustle of accomplishing and achieving. We are
introduced to the "groove stealers." Groove stealers are those people,
circumstances and things that disrupt our state of groove.

### SIN AS A GROOVE STEALER
Another name for groove stealers is "purpose prohibitors." In other
words, groove stealers get in the way of our fulfilling the purpose God
has for us. As I was pondering that thought one day, the Lord
revealed to me that the primary groove stealer is sin! I can't dress it
up. I can't make it sound pretty. SIN – when you get right down to
it, the root of most groove stealers is sin! Paul provides an excellent
example in Romans 7. In that chapter, he shares with us his struggle
with sin. In verse 24, he refers to himself as a "wretched man." The
primary groove stealer has definitely moved him off center. While
studying those verses, I realized that groove stealers can be divided
into two categories: internal and external. What Paul seems to be
describing is his war with internal groove stealers. These are often
much more difficult to recognize and address.

I find, as I conduct motivational workshops around the country, that
participants quickly identify external groove stealers.

13

For simplicity I have put them into four broad categories:

## PERSONAL RELATIONSHIPS

*"questionable friendships"*      *broken relationships*

*past acquaintances*      *strangers*

*disgruntled significant others*

## HOME & FAMILY

*divorce*      *in-laws*      *rebellious teenagers*

*marital challenges*      *ailing parents*

*infidelity*      *single parenting*

## CAREER & FINANCE

*unpleasant job tasks*      *performance reviews*

*negative work environment*      *loss of job*

*financial woes*      *mandatory meetings*

## SPIRITUAL/EMOTIONAL/PHYSICAL HEALTH

*personal illness*      *weight loss/gain*      *lonely times*

*convicting religious services*    *certain seasons*

*meal times while watching weight*

These external groove stealers are just a few examples given by workshop participants. They exist in everyone's life and are thus familiar and easily recognizable. I'm confident that if you're reading this book, you have at some time or another found yourself experiencing at least one groove stealer in either category. Groove stealers move us from our place of groove—our place of equilibrium. Often times we are not even aware that we have moved! We may feel that something just isn't quite right, but we can't put our fingers on what is wrong. At other times, the problem is quite evident, but we may not recognize it as a groove stealer.

Let's examine the broad categories.

❏    **PERSONAL RELATIONSHIPS**

Because we are designed as social beings, it is inevitable that people in our lives will impact us and we will impact them. Now, we all desire for our interaction with others to be positive, however, as you well know, that is not always the case. People who we allow into our personal space, and yes, even into our hearts are, unfortunately, the very ones who are capable of hurting us the most. I know that romantic relationships usually come to mind initially, but I want to focus on sister-to-sister or brother-to-brother or even brother-sister friendships first. Have you ever had a 'friend' who brought negative energy into your space? That person who always has a critical word or who is quick to share a pessimistic perspective. That person who can't seem to be genuinely happy when something good happens to you. That person who you know you have to watch, even though they smile in your face. That person, in my view, is a 'questionable friend.' A 'questionable friend' is one who brings confusion instead of peace; doubt instead of hope; or perhaps envy instead of joy. They may enjoy being in your presence and may even consistently seek out opportunities to hang with you. However, after a while, you find your spirit in a place of unrest in their presence. Other relationships in this category include romantic relationship gone

15

awry. People with whom you've shared love–on any level, can definitely be groove stealers once they're gone. This is particularly true when the relationship break up was not a mutual decision. In a recent workshop while we were discussing ex's as groove stealers, a lady spoke up and reminded us that current significant others can be groove stealers also. This is so true. People who are not whole within themselves make horrible partners and it is easy to get sucked into their negativity. The other personal relationship that I want to briefly mention deals with past acquaintances. Sometimes it's best to let the past remain in the past! It's funny that as time goes on, we often remember less of the bad times and more of the good times–to the point where we pick up the phone to determine if we can pick up where we left off. How often does that work? Seldom. Usually early on in the conversation we remember why that person is a past acquaintance. A good friend of mine recently did that. He and a woman had what he called a good sexual relationship, although their interpersonal interaction was rather volatile. Over time, he remembered less about the arguments and harsh disagreements and more about the good sex. Eventually he called her. Soon his brain remembered what his body had forgotten–that was a relationship that needed to remain in the past. Unfortunately, that call came with a cost, as the woman decided to create havoc in his life by making a retaliatory move. He learned the hard way and shared these wise words, "a heat check isn't worth it." (heat check - checking to see if relationships that have cooled can get hot again). The final relationship I want to cover here involves strangers. Normally, we don't think of ourselves as being in relationship with strangers. However, I include them here to heighten awareness of people who try to get in your space and as a reminder that everything that looks good to you isn't good for you–you may be looking at a groove stealer. Pay attention to any initial feelings of concern or caution.

❑   **HOME & FAMILY**
Family members, whether blood relatives or through marriage, can create groove stealing situations. Marriage is difficult all by itself, but when marital challenges are magnified by in-law involvement, infidelity, economic stress, etc., then the home environment, which is meant to be a place of comfort and solace, becomes a groove stealer. Parenting rebellious teenagers falls into this category because just maintaining the energy to deal with them is a groove stealer. Also, taking care of ailing parents, in addition to life tasks can be draining, and thus a groove stealer—no matter how much you love them or how willing you are to do all you can. Divorce and single parenting also take their toll and play their role as groove stealers—even if the situation is by choice.

❑   **CAREER & FINANCE**
Whether you work for yourself or for someone else, the task of work and the responsibility that comes with it can steal a groove. This becomes all too evident when the work environment is less than favorable or when a supervisor gives an unwarranted negative performance review. Needless to say that losing a job, no matter how bad it was, can also be a groove stealer—particularly if no other means of making a living is readily available.

❑   **SPIRITUAL/EMOTIONAL/PHYSICAL HEALTH**
When things are out of sync without and within ourselves, we are not operating in our groove. That often includes personal illness, feelings of loneliness, and being concerned with gaining/losing weight. Convicting religious services are included here because when we are living against what we believe, it is definitely a non-groove experience to listen to a faith leader speak against the very thing we are doing! Additionally, seasons impact our emotional health and are thus included in this category.

As I previously stated, identifying external groove stealers is a rather easy task. However, internal groove stealers may prove to be a bit more difficult to identify. Consider the following partial list of internal groove stealers:

**jealousy**　　**envy**　　　　　　　　**anger**　　**low self-esteem**

　　**vengefulness**　　**unforgiving spirit**　　**lust**

**pride**　　　　**greed**　　　**hatred**　　　**loneliness**

　　**emotional bankruptcy**　　　　**spiritual idolatry**

**un-confessed sins**　　　　　　**an undisciplined mind**

Look at this partial list again. Do you notice a common denominator? Look again. Do you see it yet? Underlying each of those examples of internal groove stealers is sin! Each one begins in the mind – it's a mind thing! How can I make such a claim? 1 John 2:16 provides a fundamental description of the core of sin: the lust of the flesh, the lust of the eyes, and the pride of life. Every internal groove stealer falls within one of these three categories. Let's again consider the partial list:

**LUST OF THE FLESH**
　　　　*sexual lust*　　　　　　　　　*unconfessed sins*
　　　　　*undisciplined mind*
**Lust of the flesh refers to a preoccupation with natural desires. Such preoccupation can lead to illicit sexual behavior, can keep us from seeing the need to confess sins, and can be the result of an undisciplined mind. We must remember that the idle mind is said to be the devil's playground. We must also remember that we have power over our minds. We don't have to give into the things we think about that lead us away from our place of groove. Paul reminds us in Romans12:2,"And**

18

do not be conformed to this world, but be transformed by the renewing of your mind. . ."

## LUST OF THE EYES

*envy          jealousy          anger*
*vengefulness          hatred*
*low self-esteem          loneliness*

Lust of the eyes is born out of looking at what others possess and feeling "less than," based on what we may not possess—both tangible and intangible. Such discontentment with self can lead to envy, jealousy, anger, vengefulness against others for what they have, hatred of others because of what they have, low self-esteem because of what we don't have, and loneliness born out of feelings of unworthiness.

## PRIDE OF LIFE

*pride          greed          unforgiving spirit*
*spiritual idolatry          emotional bankruptcy*

The pride of life keeps us focused on self—often to the exclusion of others. When self is the focus, it is not uncommon to be in a perpetual state of wanting more (greed). Self, operating in pride, is seldom satisfied with what it currently has. When self is the focus, it is easy to feel others are wrong and be unwilling to forgive them. When self is the focus, it is natural to use people and things for self's benefit, thus putting self's wants and desires before what God wants. When self is the focus, it is difficult to truly love or care for others, thus self will operate within a state of emotional bankruptcy. I say that because of the law of reciprocity. If we can't give of ourselves to others, we deprive ourselves of the gift of others. A continued state of not receiving emotional connection from others leads to emotional bankruptcy–we can't give what we don't have and we can't get what we don't give–it's a perpetual cycle.

From this perspective, it becomes increasingly clear how our state of mind can lead to sin. Beginning in the mind, each internal groove stealer can lead to destructive behavior. Jealousy and envy can lead to hateful behavior towards others. Low self-esteem can lead to wrong, hasty relationship choices. Greed can lead to dishonest behavior. Unconfessed sin can lead to complacency about sinning. Spiritual idolatry (putting someone or something before God) leads to a broken relationship with God. Each resulting dysfunctional behavior began as a seed thought planted in the mind. My point: internal groove stealers begin in the mind and often grow into destructive behavior.

Recognizing external and internal groove stealers is a vital step in getting your groove back. Too often we subconsciously give groove stealers power over us. When we finally realize that we've lost our groove, we blame the groove stealers. In reality, *"it's my groove and i alone am responsible for my groove."*

Careful consideration of groove stealers reveals that whether external or internal, when we allow them to have power over us, they move us from our place of equilibrium—our place of centeredness. Now, it is true that challenges, obstacles, and hard times, (whatever you wish to call them) will come into our lives – often at the most inopportune moments and disrupt our groove. We may not be able to control that. However, we can control how we respond to them! We don't have to allow challenges to become groove stealers! Whether the challenge involves finances, relationships, worries about the future, etc., God provides effective methods to deal with them. Let's consider five factors that are often identified as obvious groove stealers: **finances, relationships, holding grudges, and anxiety about the future.**

## *FINANCES*

Certainly lack of finances can be a groove stealer. I have often had more days in the month than money to cover those days. Worry about finances is something I think most people can relate to. But what can we do about this groove stealer? Start by giving your first fruits unto God—tithe! I realize this may not make sense to many; however, when we give God the first 10% of our earnings, He miraculously works with the remaining 90% to more than meet our needs! Even when it looks as if He's not working it out for your financial good, trusting in Him and standing on His Word eliminates your need to worry. Consider just a few of the Scriptures describing what God will do if you are faithful to Him:

1) **Malachi 3:10**: "Bring ye all the tithes into the storehouse, that there may be meat in mine house, and prove me now herewith. . . if I will not open you the windows of heaven and pour you out a blessing, that there shall not be room enough to receive it."

2) **Ephesians 3:20**: "Now unto Him that is able to do exceeding abundantly above all that we ask or think, according to the power that worketh in us."

3) **Philippians 4:19**: "But my God shall supply all your need according to His riches in glory by Christ Jesus."

4) **Psalm 84:11**: "For the Lord God is a sun and shield: the Lord will give grace and glory: no good thing will He withhold from them that walk uprightly."

You may be thinking, "Yea, that sounds good, but you don't know my financial situation!" No matter how bad your financial state is, it doesn't have to be your groove stealer Consider Ellen D. She's a single parent with two children. She receives no child support and started her own consulting business a few years ago. Initially, things were great; she was getting fantastic contracts and making good money—and she consistently tithed. She bought a new condo and was on top of her world. Then her financial world began to unravel. She was unable to get any contracts for an extended period of time. In her own words—she couldn't even pay companies to hire her services. Within months, her savings dried up. She eventually was able to get public assistance—but it wasn't enough to pay her mortgage. After four months of non-payment, her mortgage company initiated the foreclosure process to repossess her home. In addition, she was constantly playing Russian roulette with the electric company. She also couldn't pay her condo association fees and found herself being taken to court for that. And that wasn't all—she also owed taxes to both the federal and state government. Would you agree that she was definitely experiencing enough negatives to move her from her groove?

The only thing that got Ellen through that very tough period was her faith in God. She had learned to totally trust in Him. At one of her lowest points, all she had was $20 and she lost that at a store. When she got home and realized she'd dropped the $20 bill, she immediately called the store to see if anyone had returned it. The manager took her name and number, although neither of them really believed the bill would be recovered. Ellen cried out to God, wondering why this was happening to her. She heard the voice of the Lord speak to her, instructing her to worship and praise Him. In actuality, she didn't feel like she had much to praise God for. However, in an act of obedience, she got on her knees and began to worship God—to praise God. She praised Him for health and strength (neither she nor her son had experienced so much as a common cold in years); she praised Him for mental stability (she had not lost her mind in the midst of her calamity); she praised Him for salvation (she knew where she was going when her life on earth would end); and she praised Him for what was yet to come (she didn't know what lie ahead, but she knew everything was in His hands – and he has pretty big hands!) Moments later, the store manager called to report that her $20 had been found. Ellen knew right then, that no matter how dismal her situation was, she could trust God to bring her out. She refused to let her financial challenges mover her from her state of groove. Instead, she persevered and believed that God would honor her faithfulness to Him and turn her situation around. She also acknowledged that she had made bad financial decisions (when she had money) and asked God's forgiveness. Then she began to draft a financial plan she would follow when her money got straight. Today, Ellen has several lucrative contracts, and to everyone's amazement—she didn't lose her home. The moral of this true story? Don't allow a lack of finances to move you from your groove!

## *RELATIONSHIPS/PEOPLE*

A second common groove stealer is relationships that have gone sour. Often this happens as a result of one person saying or doing something to hurt his/her mate/spouse. Think about this: if you get worked up because of something someone else did or said, have you given that person too much power over your emotional state? I know that people we love and care for can and will hurt us with their words and actions. And please know that I am not suggesting that the appropriate response is to just sit back and allow others to misuse or abuse you. However, you are not and cannot be responsible for the thoughts and actions of others. You are, however, responsible for your thoughts and actions. You can dislike something someone close to you has done or said, but you don't have to allow their actions or words to move you to a state of non-groove. Now I'll admit this is easier said than done! To maintain a state of groove, even when you feel you've been wronged, you must first know yourself and be at peace with yourself. You cannot fully know yourself if you don't know your Creator He alone provides the "owners manual" for you. Developing a relationship with Christ paves the way for you to get to know you the way God knows you. Having a sense of self-confidence centers you so that it is not so easy for others to rock your boat and move you from your posture of groove. Even if what they say or do rattles you momentarily, when you've got your groove, you quickly return to your state of peace.

## HOLDING GRUDGES/
## ANXIETY ABOUT THE FUTURE

Speaking of peace, being consumed with memories of past hurts and worrying about present troubles and/or future challenges are the third and fourth groove stealers we'll explore in this chapter. As the saying goes, "The past is a canceled check that cannot be changed. The future is a blank check that is not promised. All that is available is today. Make the most of it!" Many of us have done something in our past of which we are ashamed. Sometimes loved ones won't let us forget the things we have done. Often we cannot forget or forgive ourselves. Holding on to the past (memories of past hurts or wrongdoing toward others) serves no purpose. Living in the past can be a groove stealer because it prevents you from being present today. A story is told of a little girl who picked up small rocks and held them in her hands every time her brother made her angry. She did this to avoid hitting him–she couldn't use her hands to hit him if she was holding rocks. By the end of the day she had two fists full of rocks. A lady approached the little girl with a belated birthday present. But the little girl could not take it because her hands were full of rocks. Did you get it? She couldn't receive the *present* because she was

24

holding on to rocks she collected in her *past*. **Today** is a present from God. What rocks are in your life that prevent you from receiving your *present*? Let go of the rocks: rocks of past hurts, words spoken in anger by a friend or loved one, revengeful actions, disappointments, anger, etc. They serve no meaningful purpose. Let go of the rocks of your past so that you can enjoy your *present* today.

It is not uncommon for people to become totally frustrated because they can't envision the future. They ask questions such as: "How will I know who is the right mate for me?" or "How will I be able to pay that bill?" or "What will happen if. . .?" Planning and giving consideration for the future is important. However, to become so focused on tomorrow that you don't live "in" today is futile. Consider **Jeremiah 29:11:** *"For I know the thoughts I think toward you, saith the Lord, thoughts of peace, and not of evil, to give you an expected end."* Whenever you find yourself becoming overwhelmed with thoughts of events that have not happened yet, or whenever you begin to question what the future holds, remind yourself of this scripture and become reassured that God has plans for you. He has given you thought – peaceful thought and careful consideration. He has an expected end or purpose for you. Now, the Bible repeatedly tells us that God is good (Psalm 107:1 and Psalm 34:8, for example). Since God is good, His thoughts must be good. If His thoughts are good, then His plan for your life must be good. If His plan for your life is good, then the expected end or purpose He has for you must be good. You don't have to know the details. You just need to learn to trust Him and let Him bring you to your "expected end."

Consider for a moment Psalm 23. For years I read this Psalm from a human perspective. A few years ago, after reading a book by W. Phillip Keller entitled *A Shepherd Looks at Psalm 23*, I realized that

David was writing from the perspective of a sheep. Looking at this favorite psalm from this perspective sheds light on the psalm's true meaning—the importance of resting in the Lord. The first 3 verses are words spoken by the Lord's sheep to other sheep who are outside His fold—words of praise and appreciation for a caring Shepherd. Eavesdrop with me for a moment as the Lord's sheep talks with a neighboring sheep of another fold:

> "Psst, hey you over there- Do you know who my Shepherd is and what He's done for me lately? The Lord is my Shepherd, therefore I want for nothing! Let me tell you what He does—He makes me lie down in nourishing pastures (You know how contrary we sheep can get) and He leads me to refreshing, still waters! (He knows where the best watering spots are!) And when I get turned upside down and discontented—guess what my Shepherd does? He restores my soul. And when I start going down a path of destruction (as we sheep sometimes do), my Shepherd gently guides me back to the paths of righteousness because I bear His name and He has promised to care for me!"

Now, while the first three verses of this psalm are the sheep talking to another sheep, the last three verses are words that the Lord's sheep speak to Him. Let's hear what's being said now:

> "Lord, I'm so glad you're with me as we tread through dangerous places; I'm not afraid because I know you're with me. The familiar sight of your rod reminds me of your power, your authority and your

26

strength in every situation. I know you always use your rod for my good—even if it is to discipline me! I also find comfort in your staff when you use it to draw me closer to you for examination, closer to the other sheep for fellowship, and to gently guide me where you want me to go.

Lord, you know where the best grazing pastures are up on the high mountains. All around me are predators wishing they could be where I am, but you've already gone ahead and prepared the tableland so that I can eat in peace. Thank you for shielding me from my enemies. And in the heat of the day, when bugs and parasites try to bury their little irritating bodies into my head, you've already anointed my head with oil that prevents them from attaching themselves to me! (I've seen how other sheep keep banging their heads against a hard surface trying to get rid of the parasites themselves)

I love you so much Lord, because with you I can be confident that goodness and mercy will always be with me. As long as I allow you to be Lord of my life, I can rest assured of my safety and well being in every situation all the days of my life!" (Keller, W. Phillip, *A Shepherd Looks at Psalm 23*, Zondervan Publishing House, Grand Rapids, MI 1970)

You see, this sheep has learned the benefits of totally resting in Jesus. Talk about getting your groove back! Oh, what peace we often forfeit when we try to handle things ourselves. You may be asking, "How can I rest in Jesus?" First, you must know Him. Because to rest in

27

Him requires trusting Him and it's difficult to trust someone you don't know. Get to know Him through His Word and through talking with Him daily. The better you get to know Him, the easier it will be to trust Him. Once you feel confident enough to truly trust Him, then—and only then—can you fully rest in Him. You rest in Him by giving Him your concerns, taking your hands off them, and believing He will work it out—without any help or assistance from you. You seek Him for guidance, but you resist the temptation to take matters into your own hands.

Consider Romans 8:28. This often quoted scripture actually challenges Christians to truly rest in Christ. Consider what it says:

> *"And we know that all things work together for good to them that love God, to them who are the called according to His purpose."*

Notice that Paul writes, ***all things***. Not some things, not many things, not some things most times. ALL THINGS. That means every situation, no matter how challenging, frightening, frustrating, etc., God is using it to work towards our good. How do we know this? Here, the Greek word for "know" is "eido" and it means to have knowledge, perceive, understand, based on past experience. In other words, we can rest in Christ with full assurance because of past experiences when He has come through! As we go through the process, (the working together) it is often painful and sometimes it may feel scary, but because we trust God's Word, we can rest—knowing that all will work according to His purpose. While each separate experience may not seem good, we can know and trust that each separate experience is part of God's bigger plan that will ultimately lead us towards the good He has for us.

## SUPERVISORS/CO-WORKERS

An initial thought may be that supervisors and/or co-workers are groove-stealers who are not easily avoided. How often do we allow people we work for or with to undermine our "center" when they say or do things that disrupt our inner peace? I dare say this happens a lot. It is easy for someone in the workplace to say and/or do things that dis-positions our inner equilibrium. After all, they may have a say so in our money. But even when a supervisor or co-worker does or says something that causes distress, we don't have to stay in our own "dark" place. Truth be told, however, sometimes we enjoy having our own pity party and may purposely stay off center for an unnecessarily prolonged time to elicit sympathy from others. Sometimes we may not know how to reclaim our "center." When this happens, our whole perspective can become skewed. Let me share another story:

> A few years ago, I experienced a situation in which one of my contracts was suddenly terminated for what appeared to be personal vindictiveness on the part of a decision maker. Since I am an independent consultant, the termination of any contract has significant impact on my livelihood. I cried. I complained to friends. I contemplated ways to avenge my "enemy." I worked myself into a frenzy in just a matter of hours. I couldn't find any relief. I was out of my groove. I remember saying vehemently, "So and so makes me so mad!" As soon as I spoke those words, I realized what I had done. I had given that person too much power. I had allowed that person's actions to disturb my peace. That was the real problem—not the other person's actions, but rather my reaction. I had given that person permission to

29

steal my groove. When I came to this realization, I
purposed in my mind to stop feeling sorry for myself
and reclaim my place of centeredness and inner peace.

So you see, not letting groove stealers take your groove is a choice.
You are in control.

As I close out this chapter, let me remind you that recognizing groove
stealers for who and what they are is paramount to maintaining a state
of groove. Do not give others permission to steal your groove. That
may even mean moving away from some people and/or situations.
People who are filled with self-hate, or who are manipulative, or who
are in a "dark" place emotionally may be groove stealers. Emotional
"dark" places include jealousy, resentment, unresolved anger, pride –
any emotion that produces negative behavior. Often people
experiencing these types of emotions want to pull you into their dark
place with them. You've heard the saying, "Misery loves company."
You don't have to go there with them—no matter how much you
care; no matter how much they try to manipulate you with their anger.
You can refuse to surrender your groove to groove stealers. You may
desire to provide emotional support for human groove stealers in your
life or point them to someone who can help them. If you can do that
without sacrificing your own state of groove, do so. However, realize
that for your own mental health, it may be necessary for you to
distance yourself from them for a while. This is not to suggest that
you leave friends when things get rough for them. However, if their
"rough place" is pulling you down, take inventory of that and then do
what is necessary for you to maintain your groove. If their state of
being brings you down or removes you from your state of groove,
what good are you to them anyway? If you are saved, you know then,
that greater is He that is in you than He that is in the world *(1 John*

*4:4b)*. That said, you can draw from the Holy Spirit within you for guidance as you pray earnestly for friends you have who are experiencing their own "dark places."

The interesting thing about groove stealers is that we often do have the power to avoid them. You don't have to give in to the groove stealers. It is a choice. You either chose to maintain your state of groove or give in to situations of non-groove – the groove stealers. Choosing to stay in a state of groove is, of course, the healthiest option. However, sometimes we readily move into a state of non-groove to prove a point, make a point, or just to be the point. Most times we are not even conscious of our movement into non-groove. We just know that we are upset about something. Choose not to let groove stealers get the best of you. It is your choice. If your groove stealer is a situation that has gotten out of control and you are feeling overwhelmed, ambushed, and totally outdone—and you feel like you are really going through—don't give in to those non-groove feelings—remember, your "right now" is not your "always!"

Effectively and successfully fighting groove stealers requires making a conscious decision to do something differently. Remember the old adage, "If you keep doing what you've always done, you'll always get what you always got." Make the decision today to stop allowing other people to steal your groove. Make the decision today to refuse to become paralyzed by that unpleasant or difficult or seemingly overwhelming circumstance in your life. Make the decision today to choose the groove-giver: the Lord Himself. Hold on to God's unchanging hand and trust Him to guide you to the other side of your "through."

31

## *REFLECTIONS*

### *Identify current groove stealers in your life:*

*Internal*

_____

_____

_____

*External*

_____

_____

_____

*People*

_____

_____

_____

### *What are you committed to doing to maintain your groove?*

_____

_____

_____

# Chapter Three:
## Watch Out for Those Groove Imitators!

*"and your laughter comes from deep within your heart – not from the tip-toe
humor of your court jester"*

*"He makes me feel so good!"*
*"I love being around her; she brings out the best in me!"*
*"The cruise I took to the islands sure did me a lot of good!"*

External stimuli are **groove imitators**. Period. End of conversation.
Things that make you feel good and people who put a smile on your
face are but momentary groove-givers. Real groove comes from deep
within. Certainly those happy types of external stimuli are good for
an emotional high and are great to experience. However, to solely
rely on external happenings to give you a sense of groove is to miss
the whole point. *"i can't   i shouldn't   and i won't depend on you
to give me my groove."*   After spending time with him or with her;
after vacationing in far away places, after having the best sex ever,
you still must return to yourself. And if you are not right with you,
your groove will remain out of reach. Many of us go through life
getting high off groove imitators. Get high off yourself and your
relationship with your Creator. Search deep within yourself and find
your groove.

But first, you've got to recognize groove imitators. Think, for a
moment, of times you have felt very bad. Now, think of what
happened externally to remove you from your feeling of funk: Did you
call a friend? Did you go see a movie? Did you read a comic book?
Did you make a "booty-call?" Did you reach for that bottle of pills or
for your favorite drink? Did you pop in your favorite motivational
tape or pick up your "positive attitude self help book?" If you did
any of  these  things instead of taking the time to search within

yourself to move from your feeling of funk, you grabbed on to a "groove imitator!" **RED ALERT!! RED ALERT!!** The thing to remember about groove imitators is that after they have come and gone, that "yukky" feeling remains – feelings of distress, discontentment, dissatisfaction, discouragement, and disorientation. are still alive and doing well!

Groove imitators look and feel like the real thing, so much so, that it is easy to confuse groove imitators with the state of being in your groove. Beware! When we are not in our rightful place in the Lord, it's easy to get reeled in by a groove imitator—particularly when it comes to relationships. Consider this woman's story:

Marilyn was college educated, had her own home and was considered by many to have it all together. She'd been married before and several years after her divorce, she began seeking God for Mr. Right. Then she met Michael. He was so fine! He had his own business, drove a fancy, expensive car, and was every woman's fantasy. To top it off, Michael said he was a Christian. Initially Marilyn wasn't looking at Michael as her possible "Mr. Right." She was enjoying her relationship with the Lord.

But then, Michael began saying all the right things. They became prayer partners and he seemed to honor her desire to be celibate. Initially, every morning they would read the Bible together over the phone. Eventually, he replaced Bible passages with "new age thinking" books. Soon their morning Bible sharing times were replaced with just regular conversation. In spite of her initial concerns and apprehensions, Marilyn slowly began to allow time with Michael to replace her "God-time" (the time she spent with the Lord). While, she wanted to maintain her celibacy, she did give in to what she

34

called "fun and frolic" with Michael—where they did everything but have sex! After a while, she began to believe that Michael might really be her "Mr. Right" – even though, deep down inside, it didn't feel right. Soon, as you may have guessed, they became sexual. Michael was an excellent lover and they got together whenever they could. Marilyn even began missing church in order to spend time with Michael. After enjoying this groove imitator for a few years, Marilyn began to miss the intimacy she used to have with the Lord. She realized she had traded true groove for a groove imitator. Eventually she and Michael stopped seeing each other.

Unfortunately, groove imitators often carry a price. For Marilyn, the price was absolute embarrassment when she received a phone call one day from the police informing her that they had in their possession video tapes secretly made by Michael of him making love with several women over an extended period of time and she was one of them. It seemed Michael had gotten himself into some trouble and the police were investigating all angles from which they could build a case against him. Can you imagine how Marilyn felt? The betrayal, the pain, the shame of it all? She soon became the topic of almost every beauty and barber shop in town. What she thought was her private life had suddenly become very public. The man with whom she had shared her love and thought she would share her life with put her in a position of open humiliation and private misery. She had been bitten and humiliated by a real groove imitator! The moral of that true story? Groove imitators are not worth it! In the words of a popular song, "Ain't nothin' like the real thing!"

Notice the progression away from groove that Marilyn took. It parallels the warnings given by the psalmist in Psalm 1. First, she *walked* in the counsel of the ungodly by allowing their Bible sharing

35

time to be replaced by "new age thinking" materials. Next, she *stood* in the path of sinners by allowing "fun and frolic" to be introduced into their relationship. Finally, she became very comfortable and *sat* in the seat of the scornful as she allowed her relationship with God to take a back seat to her relationship with Michael.

Illicit sex may very well be among the ultimate groove imitators. We can rationalize our behavior and talk ourselves into believing that what we're doing is right! Since God made us sexual beings, it is very easy to be blind to the illicit sex groove imitator. I know you've heard people say, "God made me this way" or "God's grace is sufficient." How dare us try to turn wrong into right! But groove imitators will have us doing just that. Sooner or later, the groove imitator is revealed and we find that there's a price to pay. We may not all pay the type of price Marilyn paid, but there will be a consequence for trading real groove for a groove imitator.

It is natural to turn to groove imitators to make you feel good when you don't have a healthy relationship with God and with yourself. What is a healthy relationship with God and with yourself? It is when you are comfortable with you and are totally resting in God. It is when you can truly say that you love yourself. It is when you agree with God that you are fearfully and wonderfully made *(Psalm 139:14)*, and are thus capable of choosing to move from your state of funk by reminding yourself that no matter what has happened, there is nothing that you and God cannot handle together. Having a healthy relationship with yourself and God is the foundation for lifelong groove maintenance—regardless of any painful, negative, uncomfortable situation. Groove imitators, on the other hand, provide momentary thrills and excitement. The problem is that the thrill and excitement don't last long.

### Watch Out for Those Groove Imitators!

While I was a federal halfway house administrator, I met many incarcerated people who seriously believed they had found their groove through crime and drugs! Unfortunately, they were greatly misled. A good example of a person who got caught up in his groove imitator was a young man who counterfeited dollars. He had a system that was almost foolproof and lived a lifestyle that many would envy. However, he was not a happy man. Why not? Besides the fact that his system did indeed fail him and he found himself behind bars, he was empty inside. He had the best of groove imitators: lots of money, women, cars, clothes, etc. He traveled the world in style and wanted for no material things.

But the groove imitators didn't last long. At some point he had to come face to face with himself. *"I've got to look past the superficial beyond the surface thru the screen and deep inside my shell and find my soul for therein lies my groove."* There is nothing more exhilarating than the high of inner tranquility. Groove imitators make you feel good. They make you think you look good. They, however, are temporary situations that rob you of eternal groove. In fact, groove stealers rob you of the very power that God says you have. Earlier I quoted 1 **Timothy 1:7**, "For God hath not given us the spirit of fear, but of power, and of love, and of a sound mind." Notice the first thing listed that is given to us by God is power. I'm convinced that too often Christians don't realize the power we possess through Christ Jesus in every situation! If we did, it wouldn't be so easy to be fooled and sidetracked by groove imitators. The best type of groove is feeling good about oneself and having peace within. When you know who you are and whose you are AND when you have the peace of God within, then you are capable of really operating in the place of purpose, solace, and peace that God has prepared for you! **Philippians 4:7** discloses the following promise: "And the peace of

God, which passeth all understanding, shall keep your hearts and minds through Christ Jesus."

You know you've got your groove when you cease to let small things or big things unsettle you. You know you've got your groove when you no longer depend on groove imitators to help you feel good. You're operating within a peace that passes all understanding. YOU'VE GOT YOUR GROOVE ON!   The kind of peace that passes all understanding comes from knowing who is in control. You have the choice to let GOD be in total control! Making that choice guarantees a "peace that passes all understanding." A wise woman once told me that God is a gentleman—He will not force us to make Him number one. That means that once you recognize that He is ultimately in control, and you decide to surrender your will to His, then you can rest in peace knowing that God will take care of it all – perhaps not in your sense of timing, but nevertheless, always on time.

## REFLECTIONS

*Identify groove imitators in your life.*

_____

_____

_____

_____

*When are you most likely to grab a groove imitator?*

_____

_____

_____

*How can you keep groove imitators from stealing your joy?*

_____

_____

_____

_____

# Chapter Four:
## Getting My Groove Back

*"I want to feel the wind in my face the sun on my back
a sprinkle of good fortune on my head. . .'*

There are four basic steps to getting your groove back. The steps are easy to remember thus they are easy to implement. The four steps are 1) Acknowledge 2) **R**eflect 3) **C**enter and 4) **H**eal.

At one point in my life I had a personal trainer named Marissa. At the beginning of each of our sessions, Marissa would have me stretch my muscles in preparation for our hour–long workout. Part of my stretching routine required me to 1) arch my back   2) reflect on techniques she had previously taught me   3) center myself,   and 4) heal or free my mind from toxic impurities that would hinder my progress. A similar routine proves helpful in regaining one's groove. I firmly believe that when we firmly "arch" ourselves in Christ, we position ourselves to operate within our groove.

## THE

**A** = *Acknowledge* when you are off-center and in a state of unrest. This acknowledgment is beneficial because it helps you to identify exactly where you are emotionally, mentally, spiritually, socially, financially, behaviorally, etc. This may sound easy; however, it is sometimes painful to come to terms with where you are. You may not be in a good place. In addition, groove imitators may have you fooled. Getting to a state of true acknowledgment means asking yourself some hard questions and getting in touch with true feelings. In order to get in touch with those feelings, you have got to be able to name them.

Generally speaking, we've not been taught how to do that successfully. When you're feeling sad, angry, disappointed, discouraged, lonely, unhappy, ashamed, embarrassed, frustrated, overwhelmed, inadequate, challenged, fearful, or any other feelings that generate negative energy, take time to identify your feelings and the source of those feelings. Specifically name those feelings. Then you are ready to begin to replace those feelings with more positive ones. This sounds easier than it is. It takes effort to slow down enough to pay close attention to feelings and then to name them!

I've been privy to many conversations in which persons have shared that after experiencing a non-groove moment, they were able to take the time to identify the feeling and name it. But by then, the damage had been done. They had acted out in anger or made a poor decision, or engaged in some other negative behavior. The ideal time to pause to identify what you're feeling and name it is while you're yet experiencing it. Doing so can actually serve to diffuse volatile situations or keep you from compromising positions.

The acknowledgment and naming of those negative feelings is the first of a two-phase step required to move from a state of non-groove. While acknowledging negative feelings is definitely important, part two of this acknowledgment phase is acknowledging that alone you have no power to overcome feelings of non-groove. However, "greater is He that is in you, than He that is in the world" (*1 John 4:4*). You must also acknowledge that God, your creator, is the best source of "groove-restoration." He made you and knows you best. He knows every strand of hair on your head and every thought in your heart. And in spite of that, He loves you unconditionally and wants only the best for you. That's why you can depend on Him to guide you from your state of non-groove to a permanent state of "grooving" with Him. Another "A" word would be anchor — after acknowledging that you're not in your groove, and after acknowledging that God is the best source of "groove-restoration," you must anchor yourself in Him in order to gain or regain a state of inner peace and purpose.

Some ways to anchor yourself in God include:
- scheduling prayer time with God every morning
- taking coffee-breaks with God throughout the day
- meditating on Him every evening
- thanking Him for the day's blessings every night

**R** = *Reflect* on times when you have been grounded and centered. This positions you to recall feelings of groove and envision yourself being in that mental/emotional/spiritual place again. Every time your personal equilibrium is threatened, reflect on a past moment of groove. Recall moments of serenity, peace, or tranquility. For some, this may require a period of prayer and reading or recalling scripture. Others may move into a moment of meditation. Do whatever works for you to bring to your mind a vision of groove. Remembering past blessings, past times God has opened doors, past times God has made a way out of no way, and past times God navigated people and circumstances for your good will serve as an encouragement and a reminder that if He did it once, He can do it again! The more you practice this, the easier it will become. You will find that you will experience shorter and less frequent bouts of non-groove experiences. It will get to the point where you will recognize a groove stealer and instead of giving in to that situation, you will quickly recall a moment of groove and purposely move to that state of mind.

Another "R" word I associate with *"reflect"* is *"re-frame"*. Re-framing speaks to changing your perspective. It refers to rethinking how you look at things in your past, your present, and even your future. I used to facilitate a women's group in our local jail. I often told the women that while they couldn't change their past, they could change how they thought about their past. Instead of considering past failures as dead end events, I suggested re-framing those events as life learning circumstances. I suggested that they identify lessons they could learn from their past mistakes and apply those lessons to make better decisions in the future. This philosophy can be applied to anyone. Instead of viewing yourself as a failure, view yourself in terms of your possibilities. Instead of focusing in on your deficits, identify your positives. Talk about operating in your groove! Re-framing will help you see the glass as half full instead of half empty. Since "death and life are in the power of the tongue" *(Proverbs 18:21)*, we have the power to speak either one into our own lives. The result is that we will become self-fulfilling prophecies! Re-framing negative thoughts, perspectives, and words into positive ones actually position us to experience positive, fruitful occurrences in our lives.

**C =** *Center* yourself. To move into a position of groove, you must be centered. Your mental equilibrium must be balanced. This may mean taking a quick inventory of your mental/emotional/spiritual environment to identify anything which may be inadvertently throwing off your equilibrium. Centering yourself ultimately means becoming

Christ-centered. Paul best described being Christ-centered in **Acts 17:28a**: "For in Him we live, and move, and have our being. . ." Recognizing that without Christ, you can do nothing, is the first step to being Christ-centered. Moving from that realization to craving quiet time with the Lord before doing anything else helps to maintain your "centeredness". Getting to centeredness may involve consistent times of meditation, prayer, bible study, etc. For me it involves meditating and standing on Scripture:

> "I can do all things through Christ who strengthens me"
>     *Philippians 4:13*.
> "No weapon formed against me shall prosper"
>     *Isaiah 54:17*
> "And we know that all things work together for good. . ."
>     *Romans 8:28*.
> "[Nothing] shall separate us from the love of God, which is in Christ Jesus our Lord."
>     *Romans 8:39*
> ". . .no good thing will He withhold from them that walk uprightly."
>     *Psalm 84:11*

One of my favorites which I personalize for my own benefit, is *Psalm 91: 14-15*: (This is God speaking about me)

> "Because Maxine had set her love upon me, therefore will I deliver her: I will set her on high, because she hath known my name. She shall call upon me, and I will answer her; I will be with her in trouble; I will deliver her, and honor her."

Now, before I can stand on those Scriptures, I must be doing what is stated in verse one in that Psalm. I must be dwelling in the secret place. That means I must be centered in Christ before I can realize the benefits of Psalm 91:14-15.

Taking time to center yourself daily helps you to move quickly into a state of groove whenever non-groove tries to take over. In addition, centering yourself entails embracing all of life that Jesus has for you. Notice what Jesus says in John 10:10:

> "The thief cometh not, but for to steal, and to kill, and to destroy: I am come that they might have life, and that they might have it more abundantly."

My daily prayer request is for the ability to recognize and embrace life in its abundance. The consequence of not doing this was made plain to me on a cruise I took with my daughter. The price of the cruise included a formal meal three times per day in the ship's dining room. In the dining room, elegantly dressed waiters and waitresses served us. Our food was presented on china, with crystal glassware and formal silverware. Our server placed our cloth napkin on our lap as he/she poured ice water in our glass. We could choose anything from the menu for our dining pleasure – as much as we desired. We could choose several salads, every entreé on the menu, as many desserts as we liked, and as much tea, coffee, or soft drinks as we wished to drink. It didn't matter how much we ate; the price of the food was included in the cost of the cruise. The only catch was that we had to be in the right dining room at the right time. If we missed our designated dining time, the alternative was to eat on deck from the buffet grill. There we could choose several food items that were appropriate for the time of day we were there. Now, food from the grill was good. Since it was buffet style, we could return to the grill and the soft drink machine as often as we liked. But when we ate from the buffet grill, which we did a lot, we missed out on the dining room experience. When I shared this story with a friend of mine, he quickly replied, "But the grill food is so good!" Yes, it is, but the price had already been paid for the dining room experience! My point is this, why settle for the buffet when the way had been paid for us to experience the total formal dining room service!

We do this so often in life, that we don't even realize we're doing it. We become quite satisfied with living beneath our privilege and blessings. Choosing to embrace all that life has to offer (the dining room experience) affords you the opportunity to center yourself and regain your groove. Jesus has paid the price for our salvation. He has paved the way to righteousness. He has promised peace of mind if we keep our minds stayed on Him. Why then do we enter into states of non-groove? Because we settle for the temporal or brief satisfying things life offers, instead of embracing the abundant life that God offers. Choosing to embrace abundant life is choosing to center yourself in Christ and preparing yourself to receive all that God has to offer! After all, He did promise life, and that more abundantly.

Centering yourself also involves getting to know and understand your purpose in life. We all have a purpose, but few of us come to know what that purpose is. Discovering your purpose helps to keep you centered because you will be able to focus and, in some cases, refocus your energies on what you are here to do. Not knowing your purpose leaves room for you to quickly become unfocused and rattled.

How do you discover your purpose? Identify your passion. What is it that gives you joy to do, that you do well, that you are passionate about? It may be as simple as spending time with elderly people to something as grandiose as film making. Whatever your passion is, getting in touch with it will help you stay centered and focused.

$\mathbf{H}$ = *Let God Heal* you. In other words, do the things necessary to allow God to facilitate your healing. This entails taking TIME for Him, TREATING yourself and valuing yourself as God treats and values you, and TALKING TO YOURSELF—with positive messages that God is saying to you!

> *TIME for Him*: Too often we become engaged in the process of nurturing others; of being "there" for others; of taking care of the problems and needs of others to the point of neglecting ourselves and our time with God. Take time to be by yourself and God, with yourself and God, for yourself and your relationship with God. Be your own friend and let God be your best friend. Retreat to a place and space designed and designated just for you to enjoy God's presence by yourself. Meditate, pray, read, enjoy being with you just for the sake of being with you. It is often in those quiet moments that we can feel closest to God.

A friend of mine once told me that I needed to gain a fresh perspective about God. She suggested that I begin to see Him as my lover. I took her suggestion and began waking up each morning to take time to share special moments with my new found "lover." You will never know how much that jump started my relationship with God. I began waking with great anticipation of spending "alone time" with my "lover." God began revealing things to me and sharing things with me that were profound and wonderful. My relationship with my Lord and Savior soared to untold limits. And guess what? I'm not done yet! I praise Him for His patience with me. I praise Him for the love He has for me. I praise Him for our new level of intimacy. It all came about because I dared to take time alone with just Him and me. Go ahead; you can do it. Don't be afraid to enjoy being alone with yourself and God. For often it is in those quiet times that questions are answered, problems are solved, challenges are overcome, and a light shines through your darkness.

People often miss it because they don't like taking time to do it. Dare to get into God and just bask in the thoughts He gives you. Challenge your old way of doing things. Let Him create new ways of doing old things in your mind. Energize yourself from the energy God gives you. When by yourself, take time to listen to God! In **Psalm 46:10** God speaks to us, "Be still, and know that I am God...." Notice the comma after "still." The comma indicates a pause. We are to be still. How can you be still? The perfect place of "stillness" is in Christ. To be still in Christ means to position yourself to hear Him and listen to Him. Tune out the hustle and bustle of life and seek His face: in prayer, meditation, melodies, etc. Once you are still, you will know that He is God. You can't come to a true understanding of that knowledge until you are still. Taking time for yourself provides an opportunity for refueling, for connecting or re-connecting with God.

Many of us can't stand to be with ourselves. We surround ourselves with other people, with external stimuli, with empty conversations – just to avoid being with ourselves. Let me ask you this: if you can't enjoy being with you, how can you expect others to enjoy being with you? An integral part of regaining your groove is learning to be O.K. with yourself. Go ahead – spend time alone with you and God. Contemplate your thoughts, laugh at your faults, identify your goals, see yourself as God sees you! Taking time for yourself postures and positions you to move on to the next step in the process of getting your groove back.

*TREAT* your *self*:  You deserve to be nice to you.  Give yourself a bubble bath with candles and champagne. Get your nails, hair, and toenails done. You deserve it. Take yourself to an exquisite dinner. You are worth it. Splurge on yourself sometimes – you need it. There are times in our lives when either we don't have a significant other or when our significant other doesn't treat us to the things we may want. Then treat yourself. Even if you do have someone in your life who will treat you to whatever your heart desires, still treat yourself. You need to be good to you! When I feel the need to treat myself, I may begin with a nice hot bubble bath, then follow that up with scented lotions and body sprays. Afterwards, I'll dress up in my finest, get in my car and buy myself my favorite meal at my favorite restaurant.  Or perhaps, I'll just go to a movie or rent a movie and enjoy it at home – with no one but me!  I may make that purchase that I've been putting off for any number of reasons.  I have been known to go on a shopping spree – the most expensive one ended up with my owning a new car!

You don't have to be that extravagant, but do for yourself those things that you always make excuses not to do. Go on a cruise, take a weekend trip, prepare yourself a candlelight dinner! – just for you.  If you can't be good to you, can you really expect any one else to be good to you?  Treat yourself because you love yourself. Save up for it. Plan for it. Make a date with yourself. Pamper yourself.  It's all a part of your

taking care of you. What a way to get your groove back!
God values you. The Bible says that He loves you so much
that He'll let nothing separate you from His love. (**Romans
8:37-39**) If He loves you to that extent, why not give
yourself some love? **TREAT YOURSELF – NOW!** P.S.
One of my best friends just called and told me she treated herself to
breakfast at IHOP today after dropping her kids off at a laser-tag party.
**GOOD FOR HER!**

*TALK to yourself*: I know this is not at all comfortable for
many of us. We've been told that people who talk to
themselves are crazy. Actually, you should not only talk to
yourself, but also take time to answer yourself. Let me
explain. We move through life with myriad feelings,
emotions, and thoughts. Often those feelings, emotions, and
thoughts, are confusing and may be in conflict with each
other. We hate the people we love. We lie to avoid truth, yet
we say we want truth. We become intimate with people we
don't like to avoid being lonely. We courageously run from
relationships because we lack the courage to take risks.
Confused yet? Talking to yourself provides an opportunity
for you to hear yourself out. Do you make sense? Does your
behavior reflect your thoughts? Are you being rational?

Talking to yourself can help you explore all options available
to you and you can talk yourself through various scenarios to
make a decision that is best for you. Encourage yourself
when others have discouraged you. Verbally recall pleasant
times when times are hard. Use your voice to rebuke that
voice within that tells you that you cannot do a thing. Openly
admit mistakes to yourself, but always follow with words of
esteem and love. Remind yourself out loud to let nothing

50

take your groove. Tell yourself to get your groove back and devise a plan to do so. It only takes a minute. There are 60 seconds in it, so use that quick minute to talk yourself into a state of groove. The prodigal son did it – you can, too! Of course, you're familiar with the story of the prodigal son as told by Jesus in **Luke 15:11-32**. After taking his inheritance prematurely and going away to squander his money, the youngest son of a wealthy Jewish man finds himself hungry, homeless, and unemployed. He gets a job feeding swine. After a while, as the story goes, he comes to himself and says (to himself), *"How many hired servants of my father's have bread enough and to spare, and I perish with hunger! I will arise and go to my father, and will say unto him, Father, I have sinned against heaven, and before thee, and am no more worthy to be called thy son: make me as one of thy hired servants"* **(vs. 17-19)** . The young man in the story **acknowledged** his state of non-groove, **reflected** on when he was in a better place both physically and mentally, **centered** himself mentally to make a decision to return home, and began his mental, spiritual, and physical **healing** by talking to himself, treating himself to thoughts of home, and taking time for himself to plan his return. His healing began when, under the direction of the Holy Spirit, he talked to himself. So go ahead, talk sense to yourself and change your whole way of doing things. Speak success and good things into your own life. Talk yourself into a state of groove.

Finally, let me remind you that God wants you to be healed. It is not His will that any of us live broken lives. However, He will not force healing upon us. We have to choose to allow Him to heal us. He's extended the invitation. Jesus has requested that all who are burdened

51

and heavy laden come to Him and He's promised to give us rest! Learning to rest in Jesus lays the foundation for your healing and for you to get your groove back!

## REFLECTIONS

*What acknowledgments of non-groove feelings do you need to make?*

_____

_____

_____

*Write down your reflections on occasions when you were centered. Where were you? When?*

_____

_____

_____

*Identify ways you can center yourself today (i.e. list scripture, wholesome meditations or activities, etc.).*

_____

_____

_____

*Identify how you can begin to allow God to heal you.*

_____

_____

_____

# Chapter Five:
## I've Got My Groove Back!
*"i want my groove back. . .'*

$\mathcal{I}$'d like to share a poem that has helped me rethink many options and choices presented to me. It's called "The Autobiography in 5 Short Chapters" by Portia Nelson.

### Chapter I
*I walk, down the street.*
*There is a deep hole in the sidewalk*
    *I fall in*
*I am lost. . .I am helpless.   It isn't my fault.*
*It takes forever to find a way out.*

### Chapter II
*I walk down the same street.*
*There is a deep hole in the sidewalk.*
*I pretend I don't see it.*
    *I fall in again.*
*I can't believe I am in the same place.   But, it isn't my fault.*
*It still takes a long time to get out.*

### Chapter III
*I walk down the same street.*
*There is a deep hole in the sidewalk.*
*I see it is there.*
    *I still fall in. . .it's a habit.*
*My eyes are open.   I know where I am.  It is my fault.*
*I get out immediately.*

***Chapter IV***
*I walk down the same street.*
*There is a deep hole in the sidewalk.*
        *I walk around it.*

***Chapter V***
*I walk down another street. (Used by permission)*

I often begin my workshops with this poem because it is so very fitting – particularly when positioning oneself to regain a sense of groove. You see, we often do the same things the same ways while expecting different results.  That, I am told, describes insanity.  This poem challenges us to do something different – to learn from our mistakes and chart a new course.  If you truly want your groove back, you have to begin viewing yourself, others, and life from a different perspective! To do this requires gut wrenching honesty—with yourself and God! You have got to begin dealing with the groove stealers and recognizing the groove imitators.

How do you know you're *walking down a different street* (and thus walking in your groove), as the poem suggests? Perhaps the following **Groove Barometer** can serve as a guide:

## THE GROOVE BAROMETER

- **You know you're in your groove when** your skirt falls down in the middle of your presentation, and you gracefully pull it back up and continue without losing your stride.

- **You know you're in your groove when** the person who wronged you is blessed with a promotion and you are genuinely happy for them.

- **You know you're in your groove when** a teenager with no insurance hits your car and you pray that things work out for them.

- **You know you're in your groove when** the rude salesclerk throws your change down and you sincerely wish her a blessed day.

- **You know you're in your groove when** your ex-husband, who left you to marry the woman he was having an affair with, falls on hard times and you don't gloat.

- **You know you're in your groove when** you're diagnosed with a terminal illness and decide to live life to the fullest instead of living in a pity party.

- **You know you're in your groove when** in spite of a nasty, spiteful divorce, you're able to move on with your life and maintain a positive outlook.

- **You know you're in your groove when** your husband of several years tells you he has an incurable sexually transmitted infection that he may have passed on to you and you handle your business without killing him.

- **You know you're in your groove when** your adolescent daughter's pediatrician tells you she's pregnant (during a physical exam for track and field) and you calmly consider all options and guide your daughter through a very difficult and challenging situation.

- **You know you're in your groove when** your daughter-in-law has your son arrested due to an unfortunate misunderstanding and you continue to love and support her while you raise bail money and help her care for your grandchildren—and go to court with her, pray with her, and console her while your son is needlessly initiated into the criminal justice system.

- **You know you're in your groove when** your fiancé, the man who has loved you like none other, dies suddenly in your arms and you still find reason to give God praise in the midst of your pain.

These situations have actually happened to women I know and more than one of them happened to me. We maintained our groove in spite of the current situation. Groove stealers are momentary. Real groove is ongoing despite what the "right now" looks like! What does your groove barometer indicate?

# Chapter Six:
## Conclusion
*". . .and i'm gonna get it!"*

So, do you have your groove back? It's yours for the getting. It doesn't happen overnight—indeed, it is a lifelong process that occurs in minute by minute increments.

In fact I, myself, am still in the progress of maintaining my groove constantly. Like you, I have had many non-groove moments and experiences in my life. You've read about some of them. I am Ellen D. I am Marilyn. I was sexually molested as a child. I was raped as a young adult. I was physically and emotionally abused by an ex-husband. I have looked for love and acceptance in all of the wrong places. I have been the victim of rumors and hateful actions from others. Yet I have learned to maintain my state of groove, because I have learned that my groove is not dependent on others.

As I conclude, I thought it might be helpful to summarize spiritual tactics you can utilize as you conscientiously take steps to maintain your groove when you are tempted to think and/or act in non-groove ways. To begin with, I want to remind you of Paul's words in 2 Corinthians 10:4:

> *For the weapons of our warfare are not*
> *carnal, but mighty through God to the pulling*
> *down of strong holds;*

Remember that the ultimate groove stealer is sin and sin's source is satan. It is satan's strongholds that Paul is referring to in this passage. In natural warfare, a stronghold is a mountain, a hill, a wall—anything that provides the enemy with a secure place to hide. The success of a stronghold is determined by its ability to hide, conceal, or camouflage the enemy so that he can launch a surprise attack. It works the same way in the spiritual realm. satan, the enemy, desires to have you. So, he creates strongholds in your life to hide behind so that you cannot easily recognize him. These strongholds are groove stealers and groove imitators. To be most effective in pulling down satan's strongholds, you must use spiritual weapons — not carnal ones. So here are some spiritual weapons (empowering tactics accompanied by Scripture) that you can use: (note that this list is by no means exhaustive, but does provide some tools that are ef fective in your efforts to pull down those strongholds):

1. Be on the alert for groove stealers and groove imitators. *"Be sober, be vigilant; because your adversary the devil, as a roaring lion, walketh about, seeking whom he may devour. . ."* **– 1 Peter 5:8**

2. Study the Word of God so that you can become intimately familiar with your Father and can follow His lead. (Following His lead is as important as following your partner's lead when you're doing the Chicago S tep — I know because my Step partner constantly complains that I disrupt our dance up when I don't follow his lead — don't let that be God's complaint about you) *"Study to shew thyself approved unto God, a workman that needed not to be ashamed, rightly dividing the word of truth."* - **2 Timothy 2:15**

3. Choose not to let anger get the best of you and definitely refuse to go to bed angry! *"Be ye angry, and sin not: let not the sun go down upon your wrath."* **–Ephesians 4:26**

4.  Choose to consistently operate in a state of groove instead of reacting as others may ordinarily react. *"And be not conformed to this world: but be ye transformed by the renewing of your mind. . ."* – **Romans 12:2a**

5.  Once you get to the point where you can differentiate between your groove and non-groove thoughts and behaviors, compare your choices against scripture so that you can be assured that you are operating in your groove—particularly if what you are wanting to do mirrors non-groove behavior! *". . .for satan himself is transformed into an angel of light."* – **2 Corinthians 11:14b**

6.  Practice living a lifestyle of worship by including God in everything you do and by giving Him glory in everything you do. Don't let an hour go by without thinking of His goodness, thanking Him for His blessings, or praising Him for His love. God is wanting that type of worship relationship with you. *". . .the true worshipper shall worship the Father in spirit and in truth: for the Father seeketh such to worship Him."* - **John 4:23**

7.  Don't give up easily. Know that the best is yet to come! *"And it shall come to pass in the day that the Lord shall give thee rest from thy sorrow, and from thy fear, and from the hard bondage wherein thou was made to serve. . ."* - **Isaiah 14:3**

God wants you to operate in your groove, for that is when you can best contribute to His kingdom. He made you to exist in your groove. I can boldly say that, based on creation as recorded in Genesis, chapters 1-3 and Revelation 21:4. In Genesis 1-3, Adam and Eve had no sorrow, no pain, no tears, and no fear of dying. They existed in a perfect state of groove. After sin entered into their lives (and the world), their state of groove was disrupted. Ever since, mankind has been searching to be reconciled to that state of true "groove"—by way of money, sex, relationships, possessions, status, etc.

In Revelation 21, John writes of a new heaven and a new earth. Verse 4 reads: "And God shall wipe away all tears from their eyes, and there shall be no more death, neither sorrow, nor crying, neither shall there be any more pain; for the former things are passed away ." THIS IS THE ULTIMATE GROOVE! God created us in this state of groove and will eventually, eternally, return us to this permanent and ultimate state of groove. In the meantime, we are able to experience temporal groove in Christ Jesus as we journey towards God's eternal groove. That phrase, "in the meantime", deserves further exploration. Iyanla Vanzant wrote an entire book on *In the Meantime*. The "meantime" is the journey. It is the time and space we occupy while we're moving toward the ultimate groove. It is between our "here" and our "there". Groove, then, is that place called "there" that we're all striving to reach. Remember Acts 17:28? "In Him we live, move and have our being." The application? It is only through God that we reach that place called "there" and find our groove!

Go ahead, you can do it. Get your groove back. Take back what the devil steals from you every day. After all, it's your groove, and you're gonna get it!

61